Animalographies
HeroRat!
Magawa, a Lifesaving Rodent

Jodie Parachini

illustrated by
Keiron Ward and Jason Dewhirst

Albert Whitman & Company
Chicago, Illinois

For Hannah, who loves ALL animals—JP

For Mum, Audrey, and Dad, Keith.
Thanks for the gift of Art!—KW

Library of Congress Cataloging-in-Publication data is on file with the publisher.

Text copyright © 2022 by Jodie Parachini

Illustrations copyright © 2022 by Albert Whitman & Company

Illustrations by Keiron Ward and Jason Dewhirst

First published in the United States of America in 2022 by Albert Whitman & Company

ISBN 978-0-8075-0384-3 (hardcover) • ISBN 978-0-8075-0385-0 (ebook)

Printed in China

10 9 8 7 6 5 4 3 2 1 WKT 26 25 24 23 22 21

Design by Aphelandra

For more information about Albert Whitman & Company, visit our website at www.albertwhitman.com.

Hi! I'm Magawa. I'm a rat but not an ordinary one. I'm a HeroRat! I don't fly or wear a cape, but I've saved the lives of many people, and I've even won a gold medal.

HeroRats like me are trained to sniff out land mines—bombs that have been hidden above ground or under the soil. If a person steps on the mine, or if a car or truck rolls over it, it will cause the land mine to explode.

After wars, when citizens go back to living in places where the bombs have been hidden, people can be hurt if they accidentally set off a mine. I help stop that from happening.

It's not an easy job, so we HeroRats have to
be brave and clever. Good thing I'm both.

I was born on November 25, 2014, in a training and research center in Morogoro, Tanzania, in East Africa. I've never lived in the wild.

There are many types of rats, but I'm an African giant pouched rat. Although that sounds like I should be related to kangaroos, with a pocket on my belly, the word *pouched* refers to my puffy cheeks. Like a hamster, I can store nuts and food in my mouth.

Like many animals born in dens or burrows, I was born
with my eyes shut. At five weeks old, when I first opened
my eyes, my training as a HeroRat began.

For nine months, I was trained by a nonprofit organization—a company that doesn't earn any money for the people who own it—named APOPO. I started with *socialization*, which is a fancy way to say "getting used to sounds and smells and sights around me."

MY DIARY ♥ FEBRUARY 2015

What a big world this is! I live at Sokoine University, in Tanzania, and I've spent the past two weeks recognizing things found outside my cage: the smells of flowers and plants, the glare of sunlight, the sound of trucks, the chitter-chatter of humans talking. It's important for me to know all this so I can pass my first round of training.

The other rats and I need to be tough. Being picked
up and carried by humans and wearing our harnesses
without a fuss are important skills for heroes. Any rat
that scurries away isn't chosen for the job.

The rats who aren't chosen may be given jobs such as sniffing out diseases, like tuberculosis. Land-mine-sniffing rats have to be able to focus on our tasks, even if there are loud noises or bright lights.

I passed! Next it was time for the second part of my training. For a few months, I learned through "click training." A clicker is a little machine with a button, which the trainers hold. First, they got me used to hearing a little click every time they press the button, and then I'm given something yummy to eat. Easy, right? There's another click, and here comes my delicious mashed avocado and peanuts!

Next came the TNT, an explosive used to make bombs, dynamite, and land mines. The trainers don't use explosive stuff, just pieces of paper that smell like TNT. I sniffed the paper, heard a click, and got a treat!

Did I tell you that I have a supersensitive nose? My amazing sense of smell is what makes me perfect for this job. Unlike humans, I can smell the differences among many subtle scents, even ones buried underground. I also have an excellent memory, so remembering what TNT smells like is easy, especially after the trainers used the clicker every time I came near the correct piece of paper. They even tried hiding the paper inside metal eggshells. I didn't fall for that trick!

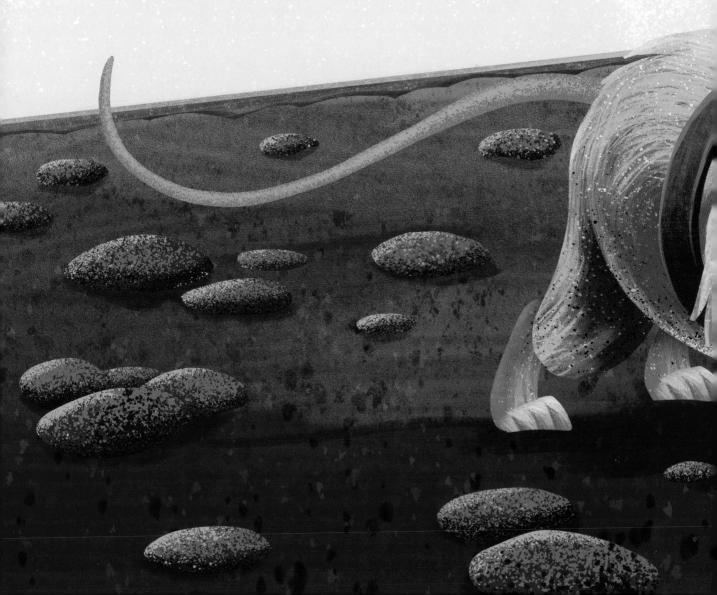

They then buried the metal eggs in dirt, in a box inside the lab. If I found all five eggs, I could begin the final test.

MY DIARY ♥ JUNE 2015

I've finally moved on to the training field. It's dusty, dry, and sandy here, but that suits me. I thought finding five eggs was easy, but the training field covers 8,600 square feet (the size of three tennis courts), and there are 1,500 objects to find! It's also more difficult, with all kinds of real land mines. Good thing they're deactivated, so none of them can explode! I have to be one hundred percent accurate, or I won't pass.

There are dogs being trained to be heroes too. But rats make better heroes for three reasons. First, we cost less to keep, feed, and train—$7,300 for a nine-month program while dogs cost $25,000 for the same training. Second, we can be socialized with more than one trainer or handler, unlike dogs, who tend to get attached to one person. And finally, rats are so much cuter (joke)!

The third reason is that rats are quick and light—I'm too lightweight to trigger the mines even if I do step on one. Some rats, like me, like to check every inch of the field, even if there are no mines hidden that day. We just love the job and always want to do our very best.

I thought it was going to be hard to become a hero, but I'm really good at searching for those awful explosives!

TANZANIA

MY DIARY ♥ JULY 2015

I'm nine months old today. Graduation day! I passed every test my handlers gave me (and ate loads of bananas!) so now I'm going to my first assignment, in Southeast Asia, 20,000 miles across the world in Siem Reap, Cambodia. I'm excited. Wish me luck!

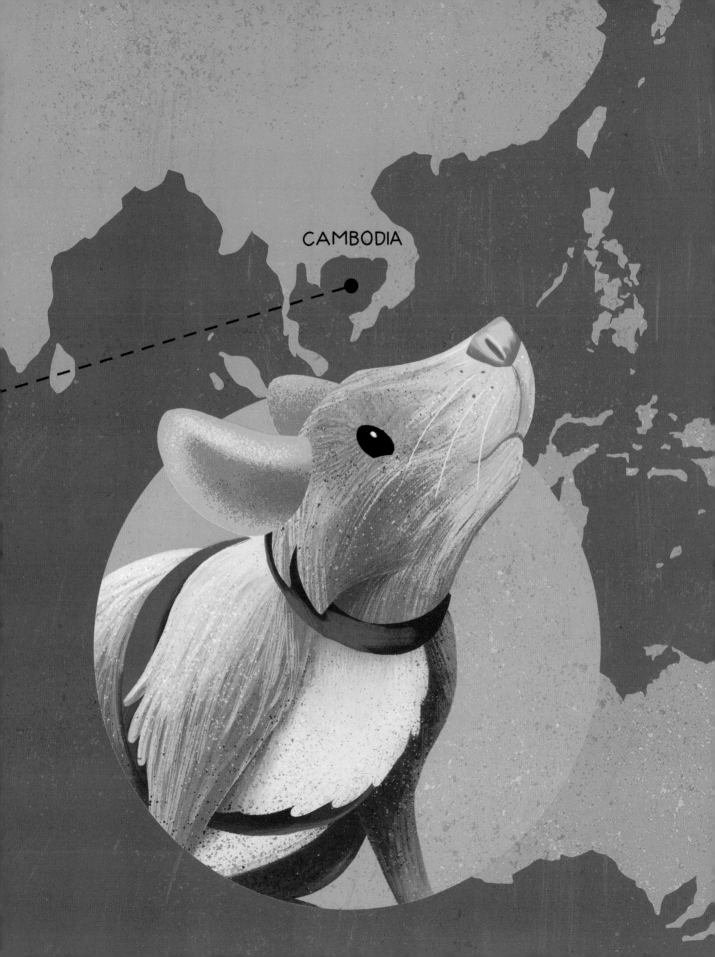

CAMBODIA

Cambodia has more land mines—about four to six million left over from wars—than any other country on Earth, except Afghanistan.

That's where I came in. I could walk across a field full of mines without setting off any, and I could sniff them out and alert people to the danger. Plus I'm really fast. A person with a metal detector would take up to four days to scan the ground that I could cover in twenty minutes, which makes me ninety-six times faster!

My new handler's name is So Malen. She's very nice.
There are nineteen of us HeroRats here, living with our
handlers. We worked for thirty minutes a day, and it seemed
more like play than work. First, our handlers put harnesses
on us and attached us to leashes. Malen held the end of my
leash as I sniffed the square of land that had been roped off.
Even if I didn't find anything, I still got a treat—easy peasy!

If I found a land mine, I scratched the earth to show Malen where it was, and a team of humans came in to detonate it safely. When we finished sniffing the whole grid of land, the workers liked to play a game of soccer on the land-mine-free ground. That's how certain they were of our success.

MY DIARY ♥ JUNE 2021

I have cleared 1.5 million square feet of land over the past five years. That's twenty soccer fields! So far, I have found seventy-one land mines and thirty-eight other explosive devices. I've been called a "bundle of energy" and a "standout sniffer." The humans think I'm the best HeroRat in Cambodia. They even gave me an award. It was gold, but I wish it was made out of peanuts instead!

In 2020, a British veterinary charity named PDSA gave me their highest animal honor, the Gold Medal "for animal gallantry or devotion to duty." For more than seventy years, the PDSA has been awarding medals to animals who have shown bravery in the face of danger. They have awarded medals to dogs, horses, pigeons, and a cat, but never a rat! That's a first! And it was the perfect size to fit around my neck. Malen attached it to my harness so I could wear it all the time.

I hope us rats can solve the land-mine problem in Cambodia in the next few years. I'm too old to go to the minefield anymore, so after helping to train some of the younger rats, I have moved to a retirement area with other HeroRats. We can eat and sniff and play all we want. Sounds good to me!

Fact Sheet

MAGAWA

African giant pouched rat
   (also known as a Gambian pouched rat)
species: *Cricetomys gambianus*
weight: 2.6 pounds
length: 28 inches including my tail
habitat: Sub-Saharan Africa
favorite foods: bananas, peanuts, and avocado

AWARD-WINNING ANIMALS

Many other animals have shown they can be brave, both during wartime and peacetime. These courageous animals have done everything from rescuing humans to calmly carrying out their jobs, even during tricky times.

GI Joe, a pigeon, won the Dickin Medal for its bravery during military conflict in 1946. GI Joe was a US Army pigeon during World War II. GI Joe flew 20 miles in 20 minutes, carrying a message that stopped the air force from accidentally bombing their own men. One hundred lives were saved.

Simon, known as an "Able Seacat," served on the British Navy's ship HMS *Amethyst*. His job was to catch the rats on board, which spread disease and ate the sailors' food supplies. Even after being injured in battle, Simon raised the morale of the wounded seamen by staying by their sides.

Sergeant Reckless, a US Marine Corps horse during the Korean War, carried ammunition for soldiers over steep terrain and transported wounded soldiers. Although she was wounded twice, Reckless made fifty-one round trips in a single day during the war, and she was loved and respected by all the soldiers with whom she served. In 2019 Sergeant Reckless won the first Animals in War and Peace Medal of Bravery.